DESERT INSECTS

North America's deserts ,
Colorado, Nevada, New Mexico, Texas and Utah, s
in the summer may exceed 110° F in the shade, and ground temperatures
can go even higher. Precipitation is less than ten inches in some areas.
In spite of these harsh conditions many insects thrive in the desert,
spending at least part of their time underground where it is cooler. Some
are nocturnal. Still others have specialized behavior and structural
modifications which enable them to move about on the hot ground in the
middle of the day.

Included in this "Easy Field Guide" are many common insects (and
other invertebrates such as scorpions, vinegaroons and spiders), plus a
few that are not so common but very interesting. Desert critters are
intriguing, not only because of their unusual adaptations to high
temperatures and little moisture, but also because many are unusual in
appearance. A number of the desert Arthropoda (the phylum to which all
the species in this book belong) have poisonous bites or stings.

GIANT MILLIPEDE

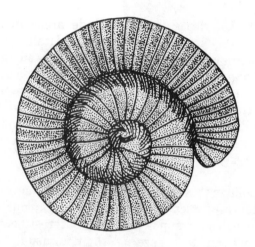

Giant Millipedes are often seen crossing highways after summer storms. Note the cylindrical form, two pairs of legs per body segment, and the habit of coiling when alarmed. They spend much time underground feeding on decayed vegetation. If handled, a strong odor is emitted and a substance secreted which can irritate the skin. Dead specimens bleach white and are often found in the desert.

GIANT DESERT CENTIPEDE

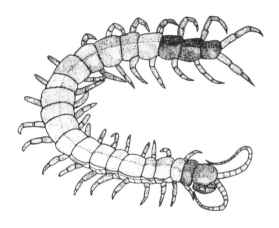

This centipede may approach a foot in length and has 42 legs (one pair per segment). It is fairly common under rocks and dead vegetation. If uncovered during daytime, it rapidly runs away. The female is sometimes found guarding her eggs. Its diet consists mainly of insects, but it has been observed feeding on mice, toads and lizards. Its bite may result in local swelling and be painful, but it is normally not serious.

VINEGAROON

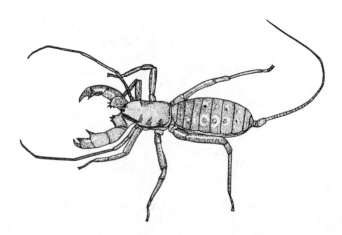

Some specimens can be four-inches long. Females carry from 20-35 eggs in a sac under the abdomen, and the young ride on the mother until their first molt. Vinegaroons emit a vinegar-like substance which contains acetic acid. They are found under rocks, logs and dead plants. The large pinchers are used to capture and hold prey which is carried to a burrow. They can pinch but are otherwise harmless. The long appendage on the rear gives rise to their common name, "whip scorpion."

SOLPUGID

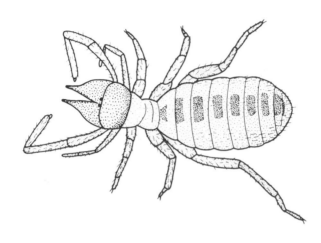

This yellowish or brown invertebrate has very large jaws. It is a rapid runner and not uncommon in houses in many desert communities. Large specimens may eat lizards, but most feed on insects and spiders. Solpugids can bite if handled, but they have no venom glands. They are also known as "sun spiders."

TARANTULA

These large, hairy spiders are found throughout the Southwest. They live in web-lined holes much of the year, but males are commonly seen traveling during the summer and early fall. Food consists primarily of insects. Tarantulas can deliver a painful bite if handled, but little or no venom is injected. There are about 30 different species in the United States. Females are long-lived, with some reaching 20 years of age.

TRAP-DOOR SPIDER

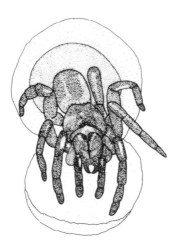

These spiders dig burrows in the ground using a spiny rake on the edge of the jaws. The burrows are then lined with silk. A hinged door is constructed, and its top camouflaged with dirt, twigs and other desert debris. The closed door is very difficult to detect. Females remain in the burrows, but males often wander.

BLACK WIDOW SPIDER

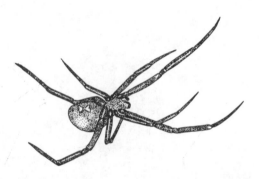

The female is distinctive, having a shiny black or brown body and usually a red hourglass on the bottom of the abdomen. The male is smaller and doesn't feed. Several egg cases are produced in a year, with each containing up to 900 eggs. The loosely-constructed webs are found between rocks, in rodent holes, wood piles and dark areas of houses. The female often hangs upside down. She produces strong venom which affects the nervous system. The female occasionally consumes her smaller mate, hence the name "Black Widow."

RECLUSE SPIDER

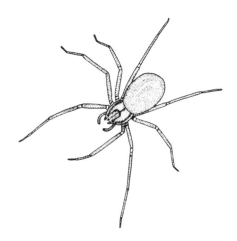

These small, dark brown to fawn spiders have three pairs of eyes and a violin-shaped design on top. Sometimes they are called "fiddleback" or "violin" spiders. They are found under wood, dead vegetation and debris. Their bite is poisonous but usually not nearly as severe in its effects as that of the Black Widow Spider. A small ulcer may form at the site of the bite.

BARK SCORPION

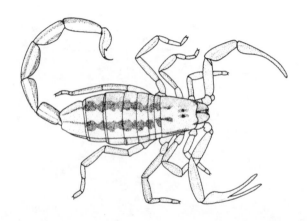

Typical specimens are about two-inches long, rather slender, and straw colored. The two dark bands on the specimen above are often lacking. Also referred to by its generic name, *Centruroides*, it has a tiny protrusion at the base of the stinger. It clings to the underside of rocks and logs and may be found in homes. The venom has a general effect on the body and may be fatal in rare instances. An antivenom is available.

STRIPE-TAILED SCORPION

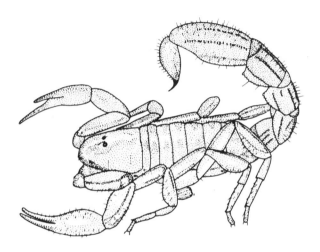

This species is larger and has a stockier build than the Bark Scorpion. It is a common ground scorpion and can often be seen in the beam of a flashlight as it scurries over the desert floor. The pinchers are used for holding prey, which consists mainly of soft-bodied insects. Occasionally it may be cannibalistic. It can sting, but the venom is generally mild with only a local effect.

JERUSALEM CRICKET

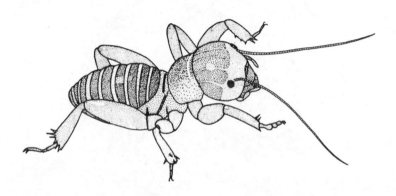

This harmless insect (it can only nip) is often feared. The dark-banded abdomen is bulky, and the large head has a wide space between the eyes. The jaws are powerful. Sometimes one will produce a weak noise when picked up. Many Jerusalem Crickets are parasitized by horse-hair worms. Navajos call it "Woh-seh-tsinni" ("Old Man Bald Head"). In some areas they are known as "Nina de la Tierra" ("Child of the Earth").

HORSE LUBBER

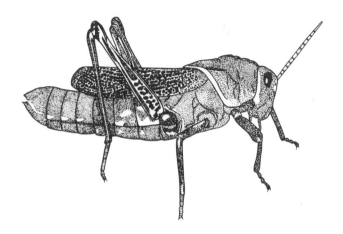

Horse Lubber Grasshoppers are abundant in some desert and grassland areas. They are often seen on roads at the end of summer or in early fall. The body is partly shiny black, the borders are yellowish, and the outter wings have a pattern of yellowish veins. The inner wings are small and reddish, bordered by black. Food consists of mesquite and other desert vegetation. We have seen them eating their own dead on highways.

PRAYING MANTIS

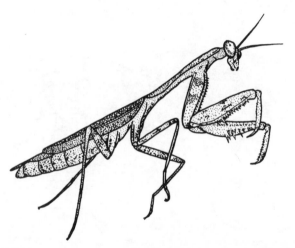

A prayer-like stance as it remains still, waiting for prey, has given rise to this insect's common name. It can turn its head, a somewhat unusual characteristic for an insect. There are many different species found in the Southwest. Colors range from browns to yellows to greens. They are harmless and very beneficial because of the large number of harmful insects which they eat. Praying Mantises are commonly found around outdoor lights at night.

WALKING STICK

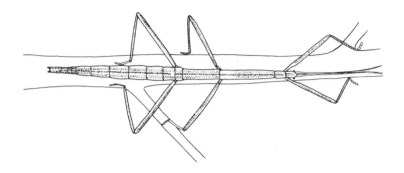

The long, slender body and legs result in this insect's resemblance to a twig. Its color often matches that of its surroundings. Females are usually stouter than males. Lost legs are regenerated in some individuals. Walking Sticks are found over much of the world, over 700 species have been described. They are plant feeders, with some species being very specific in choice of food plants.

RIPARIAN EARWIG

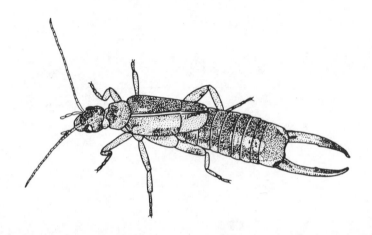

The "tweezers" at the end of the abdomen characterize earwigs. A number of species occur in our deserts. Most are less than an inch long and are often various shades of brown. They may produce an offensive odor. The Riparian Earwig is an introduced European species which is now common in the Southwest. It is a predator on other insects and is often attracted to outdoor lights.

GIANT MESQUITE BUG

Sometimes during the late summer, these large insects are so common on mesquites that the trees look like they have been decorated for Christmas. Giant Mesquite Bugs have a considerable amount of red on them—a warning to birds which tend to avoid red insects because of their unpleasant taste. This species has scent glands which can produce a strong odor. The male (above) has enlarged hind legs. Giant Mesquite Bugs feed strictly on mesquite, obtaining sap from small twigs.

CICADA

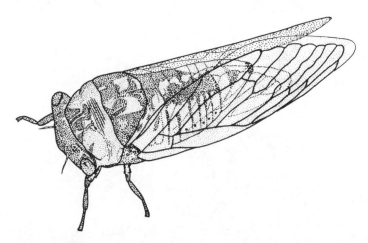

Adult Cicadas slit shrub and tree twigs and lay eggs in the slits. Nymphs hatch out and burrow into the ground where they live for several years, feeding on tree roots. (Nymphs of one northern species spend 17 years underground.) Emerging in the evening, they crawl to a perch where they shed and become adults. Adults live for only a few weeks. The presence of Cicadas in the desert is often indicated by their loud calls. Different species can be identified by their calls.

ANT LION

 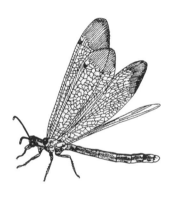

The "doodle bug" is familiar to anyone who lives in an area where there are patches of soft sand. They are the larvae (left above) of Ant Lions, and they construct shallow, cone-shaped pits in loose soils. Only the head and jaws of the larva stick out of the ground at the bottom of the pit. Insects which fall into the pit are grabbed by the jaws, and poison is injected. Body fluids are then sucked out. Adults (right above) have weak wings and narrow bodies. They are attracted to lights during warm weather.

BLISTER BEETLE

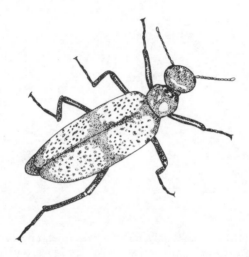

The red head and thorax of this species serves as a warning to birds not to eat it. T
abdomen is yellow and black. These beetles can cause blisters if handled. The larv
feed on the contents of native bee nests. Mating swarms sometimes occur, with lar
numbers of adults walking across the ground—hence the nickname, "soldier beetl

PINACATE BEETLE

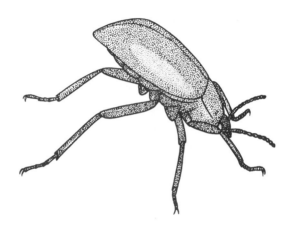

his inch-long beetle is often seen crossing roads. If touched, it may raise its rear end
nd excrete a foul-smelling substance. It is one of the more commonly encountered
esert insects. Larvae live in the soil where they feed on dead plant material.
rasshopper Mice feed on these beetles but avoid the foul substance by sticking the
ack half of the beetle into the ground. The front half is then eaten. These "half"
eetles are sometimes found on the ground.

CHOLLA BEETLE

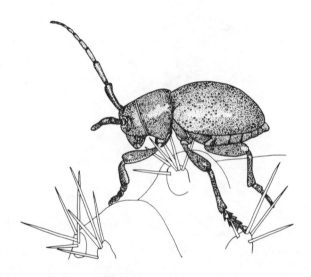

This black robust insect is also known as the "long-horned cactus beetle." I
exoskeleton is very hard, and it is flightless. The larvae feed on chollas, and adul
are often found feeding on the fleshy portions of prickly pear, cholla, and barrel cac

PRIONUS BEETLE

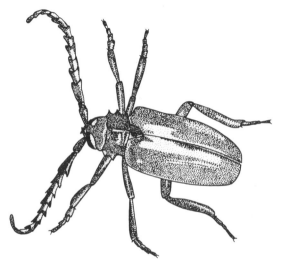

The Prionus Beetle is dark brown and about two-inches long. Note the sharp teeth on the sides of the thorax. A somewhat similar species, the Palo Verde Root Borer, is common in many desert areas. These large beetles are attracted to light and often crash into window screens with a noticeable "thud." The large larvae are found in soil and feed on roots.

MESQUITE GIRDLER

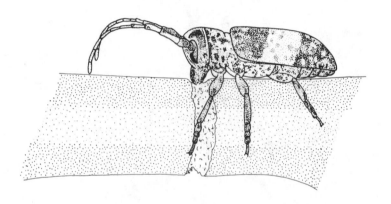

This beetle is not often seen, but evidence of its presence can be found on many mesquite trees in desert areas. Females girdle the twigs with their jaws in early summer, causing the outer portion of the twig to die. Nutrients remain, and eggs are laid in the dead, dried part—an adaptation to prevent larvae from drowning in the plant's sap. Young larvae develop in the cambium layer of the twig, but older larvae burrow into the wood.

DUNG BEETLE

A pair of these beetles rolling a ball of fresh manure across the ground can be a comical sight. These small, robust black insects are common in summer. The male and female work together to move the ball to an area where it is buried. An egg is then laid in this ball, and the larva uses the manure as a food source. Because of the method used to move the manure ball, these beetles have also been referred to as "tumble bugs."

ROBBER FLY

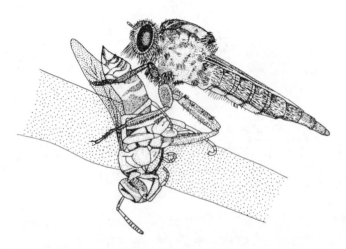

These flies are easily recognizable. They have a "hairy" face, the top of the head is indented between the eyes, and they have a long tapered abdomen. A female is shown here; males have a clasper at the tip of the abdomen. These insects are often seen along trails. Typically they perch on rocks, twigs and the like. When approached, they fly off to another perch. They capture and eat insects almost as large as they are. If handled, they can bite.

VELVET ANT

There are several different species of Velvet Ants. They resemble little dyed tufts of cotton as they scurry over the ground. Males are winged; females are wingless. Colors vary from one species to the next but include reds, oranges, yellows, golds, and whites. These insects are actually wasps, not ants. Females invade the nests of other wasp species. The sting of the female is painful, as anyone can attest after picking one up.

POTTER WASP

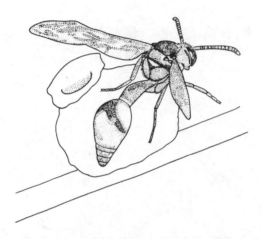

A solitary wasp, the Potter Wasp constructs a vase-like nest of clay or mud. These nests can be built in half-a-day and are found attached to walls, branches, etc. The female captures and paralyzes caterpillars which are placed in the vase. A single egg is laid on the prey. Upon hatching, the larva feeds on the still-living prey.

TARANTULA HAWK

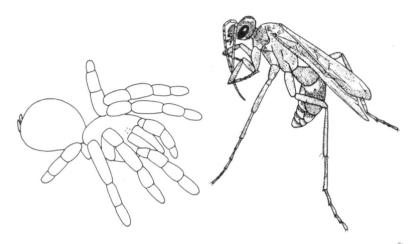

These very large wasps are gun-blue colored and often have reddish-orange wings. They dig burrows in the ground up to two-feet deep. A Tarantula is then found, stung, paralyzed and dragged to the burrow. The finding and dragging of a Trantula may occupy a Tarantula Hawk for the better part of a day. An egg is laid on the spider, and the burrow is plugged with soil. Upon hatching, the larval wasp has a good food supply.

CARPENTER BEE

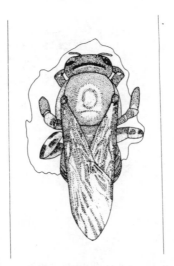

There are several species of this large solitary bee. They are most often seen when feeding on flowers. In some species, the male and female are different colors. Some males are territorial, even to the extent of chasing birds and people away from the nest area. Nests, which the female provisions with a series of cells filled with pollen paste, are built in soft stalks of plants such as agave and yucca.

CICADA KILLER

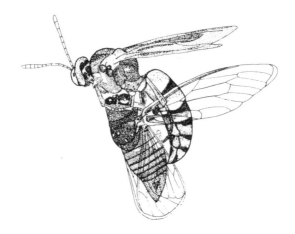

These wasps select nest sites, then find Cicadas. The Cicadas are stung and paralyzed, then transported to the wasp nest. Found in sandy areas, each nest may have several cells. Sometimes the prey is too heavy for the wasp to fly with it directly to the nest. In this case, the prey is carried to the top of a shrub, and the Cicada Killer then flies at an angle towards the nest hole. In the wasp nest, a single egg is laid on each Cicada.

CHECKLIST AND SCIENTIFIC NAMES